C.St.J. Gilbert.

A 10

Elegies

D1347862

by the same author

DOUGLAS DUNN

Elegies

faber and faber

LONDON · BOSTON

First published in 1985
by Faber and Faber Limited
3 Queen Square London WC1N 3AU

Reprinted in 1985 and 1986 (four times)

Filmset by Wyvern Typesetting Ltd Bristol
Printed in Great Britain by
Redwood Burn Ltd
Trowbridge Wilts

All rights reserved

© Douglas Dunn, 1985

This book is sold subject to the condition that it shall not,
by way of trade or otherwise, be lent, resold, hired out or
otherwise circulated without the publisher's prior consent
in any form of binding or cover other than that in which
it is published and without a similar condition including
this condition being imposed on the subsequent purchaser

British Library Cataloguing in Publication Data

Dunn, Douglas
Elegies
I. Title
821'.914   PR6054.U54

ISBN 0–571–13570–6
ISBN 0–571–13469–6 Pbk

In memoriam
LESLEY BALFOUR DUNN
1944–1981

Salute, o genti umane affaticate!
Tutto trapassa e nulla può morir.
Noi troppo odiammo e sofferimmo. Amate.
Il mondo è bello e santo è l'avvenir.

Carducci

Acknowledgements are made to the editors of the following periodicals: *Encounter; Gallimaufry; Glasgow Herald; London Magazine; London Review of Books; New Statesman; The New Yorker; Observer; Poetry Book Society Supplements; Poetry Review; Quarto; Smoke; Thames Poetry.*

Contents

Re-reading Katherine Mansfield's
Bliss and Other Stories

A pressed fly, like a skeleton of gauze,
Has waited here between page 98
And 99, in the story called "Bliss",
Since the summer of '62, its date,

Its last day in a trap of pages. Prose
Fly, what can "Je ne parle pas français" mean
To you who died in Scotland, when I closed
These two sweet pages you were crushed between?

, Bizarre image.

Here is a green bus ticket for a week
In May, my place mark in "The Dill Pickle".
I did not come home that Friday. I flick
Through all our years, my love, and I love you still.

Confession of deceit or affirmation of love?

These stories must have been inside my head
That day, falling in love, preparing this
Good life; and this, this fly, verbosely buried
In "Bliss", one dry tear punctuating "Bliss".

Love has an end.

The Butterfly House

I want a normal life, with wallpaper, and bookends.
Adelaide, in *Guys and Dolls*

Slow traffic ticks, heedful of ice and children.
I have come home with catfood, cabbage, beef,
Apples and tangerines, and with wet feet.
I am sitting within my own address,
My house, post-coded by the GPO,
A citizen within the audience
Administered by HM Government,
Hull District Council, the Inland Revenue,
North-Eastern Gas, Yorkshire Electricity.
Smiled at by the newscaster now, later
The Met Man will turn to face me, clearing
His throat, his snow sign placed above the Humber.
As I draw the curtains, this, I tell myself,
Is how it feels to be at home, waiting
For my love's car, its headlamps on the house,
The garage door with its familiar groan.
Our lives are decorated, too, by paint,
Wallpaper, books and prints, by furniture
Chosen on principle to please more than
The eye – these chairs: wooden philosophers
Considering the artistry of trees;
That fabric on the sofa, that bronze frog,
That strangely Egyptian metronome,
Are objects implicated in my love
And, like my Anglepoise, moments of me
And moments of my love and me together,
And her moments, her secret visions in them.
Fruit in the bowl is good abundance, cold
In the palm of a hand, four countries there –
Producido en España, Fyffe's bananas,

Moroccan oranges, the demotic apple.
This room is everywhere, in its pictures,
Its minerals and chemistry, its woods,
Its weeping fig, bamboos, its foreign stuffs,
That slave trade in its raw materials.
But timbers long for unfootprinted forests,
China was baked from clay, metals from earth,
And these tame plants were stolen from the ground.
There's Fujiyama, white on cloisonné,
Manhattan water-coloured in the 1920s,
A girl at Spurn, the Clyde, Lord's Cricket Ground.
These books are bound in skins of animals.
The cruelties of comfort know no end
And good taste eats the properties of world
To make a world, a viewpoint of the heart.
A stained-glass butterfly adorns my window.
Blue, green, red and yellow it is, surreal
It is also. I call this The Butterfly House.
It is alive in all its bits and pieces,
Organic, and inorganic, breathing together.
At night our spirits fly on dusty wings,
Lepidopterous, antennae'd souls.
And that is why I feel at home, but feel
That the large percentage of me that is water
Is conspiring to return to the sea,
Or to the river, flowing in its own shapes,
It, too, alive in the long room of its being.

Second Opinion

We went to Leeds for a second opinion.
After her name was called,
I waited among the apparently well
And those with bandaged eyes and dark spectacles.

A heavy mother shuffled with bad feet
And a stick, a pad over one eye,
Leaving her children warned in their seats.
The minutes went by like a winter.

They called me in. What moment worse
Than that young doctor trying to explain?
"It's large and growing." "What is?" "Malignancy."
"Why *there*? She's an artist!"

He shrugged and said, "Nobody knows."
He warned me it might spread. "Spread?"
My body ached to suffer like her twin
And touch the cure with lips and healing sesames.

No image, no straw to support me – nothing
To hear or see. No leaves rustling in sunlight.
Only the mind sliding against events
And the antiseptic whiff of destiny. ~ *cleans away all hope*

Professional anxiety –
His hand on my shoulder
Showing me to the door, a scent of soap,
Medical fingers, and his wedding ring.

Thirteen Steps and the Thirteenth of March

She sat up on her pillows, receiving guests.
I brought them tea or sherry like a butler,
Up and down the thirteen steps from my pantry.
I was running out of vases.

More than one visitor came down, and said,
"Her room's so cheerful. She isn't afraid."
Even the cyclamen and lilies were listening,
Their trusty tributes holding off the real.

Doorbells, shopping, laundry, post and callers,
And twenty-six steps up the stairs
From door to bed, two times thirteen's
Unlucky numeral in my high house.

And visitors, three, four, five times a day;
My wept exhaustions over plates and cups
Drained my self-pity in these days of grief
Before the grief. Flowers, and no vases left.

Tea, sherry, biscuits, cake, and whisky for the weak . . .
She fought death with an understated mischief –
"I suppose I'll have to make an effort" –
Turning down painkillers for lucidity.

Some sat downstairs with a hankie
Nursing a little cry before going up to her.
They came back with their fears of dying amended.
"Her room's so cheerful. She isn't afraid." Hollow comfort.

[13]

Each day was duty round the clock.
Our kissing conversations kept me going,
Those times together with the phone switched off,
Remembering our lives by candlelight.

John and Stuart brought their pictures round,
A travelling exhibition. Dying,
She thumbed down some, nodded at others,
An artist and curator to the last,

Honesty at all costs. She drew up lists,
Bequests, gave things away. It tore my heart out.
Her friends assisted at this tidying
In a conspiracy of women.

At night, I lay beside her in the unique hours.
There were mysteries in candle-shadows,
Birds, aeroplanes, the rabbits of our fingers,
The lovely, erotic flame of the candlelight.

Sad? Yes. But it was beautiful also.
There was a stillness in the world. Time was out
Walking his dog by the low walls and privet.
There was anonymity in words and music.

She wanted me to wear her wedding ring.
It wouldn't fit even my little finger.
It jammed on the knuckle. I knew why.
Her fingers dwindled and her rings slipped off.

After the funeral, I had them to tea and sherry
At the Newland Park. They said it was thoughtful.
I thought it was ironic – one last time –
A mad reprisal for their loyalty.

Arrangements

"Is this the door?" This must be it. No, no.
We come across crowds and confetti, weddings
With well-wishers, relatives, whimsical bridesmaids.
Some have happened. Others are waiting their turn.
One is taking place before the Registrar.
A young groom is unsteady in his new shoes.
His bride is nervous on the edge of the future.
I walk through them with the father of my dead wife.
I redefine the meaning of "strangers".
Death, too, must have looked in on our wedding.
The building stinks of municipal function.
"Go through with it. You have to. It's the law."
So I say to a clerk, "I have come about a death."
"In there," she says. "You came in by the wrong door."

A woman with teenaged children sits at a table.
She hands to the clerk the paper her doctor gave her.
"Does that mean 'heart attack'?" she asks.
How little she knows, this widow. Or any of us.
From one look she can tell I have not come
With my uncle, on the business of my aunt.
A flake of confetti falls from her fur shoulder.
There is a bond between us, a terrible bond
In the comfortless words, "waste", "untimely", "tragic",
Already gossiped in the obit. conversations.
Good wishes grieve together in the space between us.
It is as if we shall be friends for ever
On the promenades of mourning and insurance,
In whatever sanatoria there are for the spirit,
Sharing the same birthday, the same predestinations.
Fictitious clinics stand by to welcome us,
Prefab'd and windswept on the edge of town

Or bijou in the antiseptic Alps,
In my case the distilled clinic of drink,
The clinic of "sympathy" and dinners.

We enter a small office. "What relation?" he asks.
So I tell him. Now come the details he asks for.
A tidy man, with small, hideaway handwriting,
He writes things down. He does not ask,
"Was she good?" Everyone receives this Certificate.
You do not need even to deserve it.
I want to ask why he doesn't look like a saint,
When, across his desk, through his tabulations,
His bureaucracy, his morbid particulars,
The local dead walk into genealogy.
He is no cipher of history, this one,
This recording angel in a green pullover
Administering names and dates and causes.
He has seen all the words that end in -oma.
"You give this to your undertaker."

When we leave, this time it is by the right door,
A small door, taboo and second-rate.
It is raining. Anonymous brollies go by
In the ubiquitous urban drizzle.
Wedding parties roll up with white ribbons.
Small pools are gathering in the loving bouquets.
They must not see me. I bear a tell-tale scar.
They must not know what I am, or why I am here.
I feel myself digested in statistics of love.

Hundreds of times I must have passed this undertaker's
Sub-gothic premises with leaded windows,
By bus, on foot, by car, paying no attention.
We went past it on our first day in Hull.
Not once did I see someone leave or enter,
And here I am, closing the door behind me,
Turning the corner on a wet day in March.

A Silver Air Force

They used to spin in the light, monoplanes,
Biplanes, a frivolous deterrent to
What had to happen. Silver-winged campaigns,
Dogfights against death, she blew, and I blew,
The mobile spun: Faith, Hope and Charity,
Wing and a Prayer, shot down, shot down in flames.
I watched, and thought, "What will become of me
When she is dead?" I scramble in my dreams
Again, and see these secret Spitfires fly
As the inevitable aces of the sky,
Hanging from threads, a gentle violence.
But day by day they fell, and each plane crashed
On far, hereafter wheatfields in God's distance –
White strings of hope a summer blueness washed.

France

A dozen sparrows scuttled on the frost.
We watched them play. We stood at the window,
And, if you saw us, then you saw a ghost
In duplicate. I tied her nightgown's bow.
She watched and recognized the passers-by.
Had they looked up, they'd know that she was ill –
"Please, do not draw the curtains when I die" –
From all the flowers on the windowsill.

"It's such a shame," she said. "Too ill, too quick."
"I would have liked us to have gone away."
We closed our eyes together, dreaming France,
Its meadows, rivers, woods and *jouissance*.
I counted summers, our love's arithmetic.
"Some other day, my love. Some other day."

The Kaleidoscope

To climb these stairs again, bearing a tray,
Might be to find you pillowed with your books,
Your inventories listing gowns and frocks
As if preparing for a holiday.
Or, turning from the landing, I might find
My presence watched through your kaleidoscope,
A symmetry of husbands, each redesigned
In lovely forms of foresight, prayer and hope.
I climb these stairs a dozen times a day
And, by that open door, wait, looking in
At where you died. My hands become a tray
Offering me, my flesh, my soul, my skin.
Grief wrongs us so. I stand, and wait, and cry
For the absurd forgiveness, not knowing why.

Sandra's Mobile

A constant artist, dedicated to
Curves, shapes, the pleasant shades, the feel of colour,
She did not care what shapes, what red, what blue,
Scorning the dull to ridicule the duller
With a disinterested, loyal eye.
So Sandra brought her this and taped it up –
Three seagulls from a white and indoor sky –
A gift of old artistic comradeship.
"Blow on them, Love." Those silent birds winged round
On thermals of my breath. On her last night,
Trying to stay awake, I saw love crowned
In tears and wooden birds and candlelight.
She did not wake again. To prove our love
Each gull, each gull, each gull, turned into dove.

Birch Room

Rotund and acrobatic tits explored
Bud-studded branches on our tallest birch tree,
A picture that came straight from her adored,
Delightfully composed chinoiserie.

She was four weeks dead before that first
Green haunting of the leaves to come, thickening
The senses with old hopes, an uncoerced
Surrender to the story of the Spring.

In summer, after dinner, we used to sit
Together in our second floor's green comfort,
Allowing nature and her modern inwit
Create a furnished dusk, a room like art.

"If only I could see our trees," she'd say,
Bed-bound up on our third floor's wintry height.
"Change round our things, if you should choose to
                                         stay."
I've left them as they were, in the leaf-light.

Writing with Light

A *dadaiste* tomboy, she'd fill a jar
Then hold it to the sun. The art of day
Leapt on the shapely glass, the unfamiliar
Blues, changes, clouds, a watery display
That calmed and caught clear heavens in a jar.

And damn the hand-washing. She'd run the tap,
Filling her jar, then hold it to the sun.
That contemplated water formed a trap
To catch the sky with. Experimental fun –
A jar, a sky, the flowing cold, a tap.

Mischievous girl – but she would dress so well.
I'd see from out our bamboo bed of love
Her fine unfolded clothes heaped where they fell,
And shoes, a hat, a stray unpartnered glove,
Discarded earrings, for she dressed so well.

And as for art, then she could write with light,
A rational, surreal photography
Reconjuring a world in black and white –
A pond in a box, a tabletop of sea.
I see her in the dark, writing with light.

Best friend and love, my true contemporary,
She taught me how to live, then how to die,
And I curate her dreams and gallery.
Writing with light, the heart within my eye
Shines on my grief, my true contemporary.

Attics

A room, unutterably feminine,
A room she dreamed, but painted by Gwen John –
I see a white-distempered attic in
Her mind, pastel, and faintly put-upon
By men, who cannot understand the light
From the window, lingering on the lace
Curtain's folds, or the disturbing woman-white
Illumination on the mirror, almost a face.
A girl is sitting on a fragile chair
With her sad brushes and her thoughts, her hair
In tints of autumn, and her skin says, *Kiss,*
Kiss, kiss my skin, for I am touch and sense
Brushed womanly into this eloquence,
Unclothed in paint to teach you nakedness.

The Stranger

I pass the eccentric victim who sits
Outside the Gallery in which she worked.
He is a bottle tramp, but dapper in
His shabbily outworn man-of-the-world
Bits and pieces of clothes, his wide-brimmed hat,
The leather string of his tie. Vaguely Latin,
Or breezed in from pre-war Venezuela,
He sits there reading last night's *Hull Daily Mail*.
He looks like a placemark in history,
A refugee from what he did, or did
Not choose, familiar of the British roads.
They were on the terms of "Good morning".
She was interested in his mystery,
Telling me how he did not congregate
With the rope-belted, the tyre-shod bibbers,
Those who wait at the foot of the statue
With their packages and flaunted bottles.
He, too, knows of the young woman who said
"Good morning" to him, and he has mourned
The loss of a civil greeting, a large
Silence among the many in which he lives.
He nods to me; I nod to him. "And now
You too shall know the comfort of small mercies.
No citizen but flees from private truth,
For all their attachments, the giving of love."

Tursac

Her pleasure whispered through a much-kissed smile.
"Oh, rock me firmly at a gentle pace!"
My love had lusty eagerness and style.
Propriety she had, preferring grace
Because she saw more virtue in its wit,
Convinced right conduct should have glamour in it
Or look good to an educated eye,
And never more than in those weeks of France
Perfected into rural elegance,
Those nights in my erotic memory.
I call that little house our *Thébaïde*
(The literary French!), and see her smile,
Then hear her in her best sardonic style:
"Write out of me, not out of what you read."

Dining

No more in supermarkets will her good taste choose
   Her favourite cheese and lovely things to eat,
Or, hands in murmuring tubs, sigh as her fingers muse
   Over the mundane butter, mundane meat.
Nor round the market stalls of France will Lesley stroll
   Appraising aubergines, *langoustes*, *patisseries*
And artichokes, or hear the poultry vendors call,
   Watch merchants slicing spokes in wheels of Brie.
My lady loved to cook and dine, but never more
   Across starched linen and the saucy pork
Can we look forward to *Confit de Périgord*.
   How well my lady used her knife and fork!
Happy together – ah, my lady loved to sport
   And love. She loved the good; she loved to laugh
And loved so many things, infallible in art
   That pleased her, water, oil or lithograph,
With her own talent to compose the world in light.
   And it is hard for me to cook my meals
From recipes she used, without that old delight
   Returning, masked in sadness, until it feels
As if I have become a woman hidden in me –
   Familiar with each kitchen-spotted page,
Each stain, each note in her neat hand a sight to spin me
   Into this grief, this kitchen pilgrimage.
O my young wife, how sad I was, yet pleased, to see
   And help you eat the soup that Jenny made
On your last night, who all that day had called for tea,
   And only that, or slept your unafraid,
Serene, courageous sleeps, then woke, and asked for tea –
   "Nothing to eat. Tea. Please" – lucid and polite.
Eunice, Daphne, Cresten, Sandra, how you helped me,
   To feed my girl and keep her kitchen bright.

Know that I shake with gratitude, as, Jenny, when
　　My Lesley ate your soup on her last night,
That image of her as she savoured rice and lemon
　　Refused all grief, but was alight
　　With nature, courage, friendship, appetite.

Empty Wardrobes

I sat in a dress shop, trying to look
As dapper as a young ambassador
Or someone who'd impressed me in a book,
A literary rake or movie star.

Clothes are a way of exercising love.
False? A little. And did she like it? Yes.
Days, days, romantic as Rachmaninov,
A ploy of style, and now not comfortless.

She walked out from the changing-room in brown,
A pretty smock with its embroidered fruit;
Dress after dress, a lady-like red gown
In which she flounced, a smart career-girl's suit.

The dress she chose was green. She found it in
Our clothes-filled cabin trunk. The pot-pourri,
In muslin bags, was full of where and when.
I turn that scent like a memorial key.

But there's that day in Paris, that I regret,
When I said No, franc-less and husbandly.
She browsed through hangers in the Lafayette,
And that comes back tonight, to trouble me.

Now there is grief the couturier, and grief
The needlewoman mourning with her hands,
And grief the scattered finery of life,
The clothes she gave as keepsakes to her friends.

The Sundial

You stood with your back to me
By that crumbling sundial,
Leaving your book on it –
Time, love and literature!
You shielded your eye from the sun
As a peacock strutted towards you.
You called it beautiful and touched its head,
Then turned around to me, eye-patched
And fastened to a mourning blink
Brought there by melanoma's
Sun-coaxed horrific oncos,
Leaving me to guess at
What mysteries you knew
Foretold by love or creatures.

At Cruggleton Castle

The trees stepped back into a giant mist.
A razorbill was a little lookout
In the binoculars, alone on its ledge.
Green, blue and yellow, the Bay dealt
Its sunken mirrors under the little boats
In a shuffle of sea-glass.
A Gallovidian palette, colourist,
Gathered its greeny pinks and evening blues
From the light in the middle of our lives.
Good minutes make good days. Good days make years.
A breeze dried on my lips; the Solway slapped
Against the cliffs of Cruggleton.
Wind in her hair, the wind composing her;
The wind entangled in her summer dress
Flew from her over the land, womanly.
Doves in a kirkyard slumbered on the stones.
That dusk was pure, pictorial, painterly,
An innocence, a loss, a life away.

Château d'If

Her photographs of white embrasures glow
Against impossible blue, the sea and sky
Contemptuous of how men fortify
The State's iniquity. I do not know
Exactly all we talked about or did.
I was wearing my blue jacket, my off-white
French slacks. She posed me as a blue vignette –
"Lean on these battlements, then turn your head."
I can't remember, but I can't forget
Our outing to the Château d'If, kept now
In these rectangles of a printed light,
Other than that she liked the day, and how
She said she'd read that book of martyrdom.
"Let's stay awhile, then take the last boat home."

Creatures

A lime tree buzzed with its remembered bees.
We stood on the terrace. Fanatic prayers
Rattled with resigned displeasure. Martyrs!
"Ave!" Grasshoppers. Insect rosaries.

Nervously proud, itself, and secular,
A fox patrolled on its instinctive route
Past us and nut trees to the absolute
Wild pathless woods, a French fox, pure *renard*.

Hérisson and the encyclopaedic owl
Plotted the earth and sky of dusk. Oldest
Inhabited valley – we felt it blessed
By creatures and impacted human soul.

She said, "The world is coming out tonight."
Vézère's *falaises* moved grey; an ivied mist
Disguised the distance and we stood, our trust
In lizards, settling birds, the impolite

Belettes, the heavy hornets and the truths
Compiling in our senses, plain, of this life,
If inarticulate. I loved my wife.
Our two lives fluttered like two windowed moths.

She was the gentlest creature of them all.
She scattered milk-dipped bread for the lazy snakes
Asleep in the Mouliniers' bramble-brakes.
I asked her, "Why?" "It's only natural."

A paradisal stasis filled the dark.
She scattered bread. "A snake's a shy creature."
I dip my bread in milk, and I think of her,
The châtelaine of her reasonable ark.

Pretended Homes

I am returning to that treeless drama
Where rock and sea and passionate distances
Invent an island. Ground and air congeal
Around phenomena that happen here.
A nightclub, penthoused high up on The Paps,
Is lit with pleasurable trivia.
Sheep graze up to its doors. The fishermen,
The electrician and the butcher's boy
Play Punto Banco in a private alcove.
The cinema, down on the tideline,
Is managed by a sour projectionist
In love with Myrna Loy. He lives his life
In the black-and-white of a standard flea-pit.
And this is an island of blind fiddlers
Where storytellers speak by pulsing oil-lamps,
Telling of kelpies and brownies, of the man
Who wed his spirit-sweetheart, under the hill.
I am making a place to the song of
Sorrow and wind and the man-eating seas
That writes itself on the guitars of marram,
On Aeolian dunes, on rippled sifts of the strand.
I am making my heart, wondering why
It pictures glamour in a wilderness,
And *glamourie*, Ovidian and Gaelic.
   The sea-circus is coming on its strange boats
With its elephants, clowns and saxophones,
With boxes of sawdust and baled canvas,
Its coils of rope, with its fire-eaters.
White ponies are hollow-hoofed on the jetty.
The harbour-master's wife sits at her mirror.
Lions and tigers in their wheeled cages
Displace the latitudes; the acrobats

Tumble and leap outside the bars. Already
The postman's daughter is in love with a
Blond boy who somersaults without a net
From a trembling swing. We will be there tonight
In all our finery, to watch the clowns
On their monobikes, and the seals that slip
Obediently out of our local seas,
And the lions, with their big teeth, zebras
In African stripes. Here is a conch. Listen
To the sea. It is the music of your love,
Whoever you care for. And this is also
A land of the uncomplicated sabbath
Where nothing happens on a Sunday other
Than dawn, the day, and simple pagan prayers,
A spreading of the charitable crumbs,
A bowl of curds and whey for the good neighbours,
The aborigines of these islands.
    The weary scholars in the Library
Have mastered everything there is to know.
Soon they'll begin their study of the sea
And sky, the physics of the open-winged
Feathery sea-eagle, and, when they have learned
To fly, the deities of the blue wind,
The black wind and the blow laden with rain.
Tonight these academic bachelors
Will dress for dinner and attend *Le Cirque*
De la Mer Bleue, come from Armorica
To fall in love with us and break our hearts.
For they are the servants of the sea, brought
On the happiness of a calm ocean,
Horizon after horizon, and over
Wet hills when the sun sets, like the whole world
Going down in its sufferings of pink,
Red, yellow, dark, and the light dimmed every day,
Complete and universal, wise and good

No matter present grief hurting your heart.
  From this real house, I go beyond myself
Into imagined clarity, sorting
It out. I see her where the shingle sings
With salt, looking for pretty stones, her skirt
Held out of water's sea-lazy stroke and surge.
I am inventing here for one who's dead.
I am making a place for her. It is
On no map. It is out of my spirit.
Clowns, acrobats, a braided orchestra,
A zoo led by remembering elephants –
Their gaiety comes on a fictitious fleet
To play with northern marvels, which are sky,
Sea, rock, the pale sand an accordion
Crooning the wind and sifting its own sieves.
I wave; I shout. The cold sun sips the ocean.
I make a flat stone skid across the sea
And all my calling cannot bring her back
To this real house, she in so much of it.
Its artistry is cooling from her touch –
The yellow sideboards and ceramic boats,
Her miniatures, her objects for the hand,
A poetry of rooms spun from her heart.
So close, my love. Our dreams are cooling too.   — *ultimate end.*
We go beyond ourselves, beyond our deaths.

At the Edge of a Birchwood

Beneath my feet, bones of a little bird
Snap in a twig-flutter. A hundred wings
Adore its memory, and it is heard
In the archival choirs now where it sings.

Ewes nurse their lamb-flock on an upland field.
Late gambols in the last kick of the sun
As I scoop dirt on a hand's weight, briefly held,
A cradled cup of feathered, egg-shelled bone,

Turning the earth on it; and underground
Go song and what I feel, go common things
Into the cairn of a shoe-patted mound,
Goes half my life, go eyes, instinct and wings.

The moon rubs through the blue pallor of high east
And childlessness has no number in the May
Shadowed with birchlight on the county's crest.
This year her death-date fell on Mother's Day.

Larksong

A laverock in its house of air is singing
May morning, May morning, and its trills drift
High on the flatland's abstract hill
In the down-below of England.
I am the aerial photograph it takes of me
On a sonar landscape
And it notates my sorrow
In Holderness, where summer frost
Melts from the green like her departing ghost.

The Clear Day

Sunlight gathers in the leaves, dripping
Invisible syrups. Long afternoons
Have been reduced to this significant
Table, melodious ice cubes shaken in
A blue tumbler, lazily tipped vermouth
And a hand measuring it, a propped elbow,
A languid eye, while a reflection on
A leaf turns into everything called summer.
The heat haze ripples through the far away
Gardens of strangers, acquaintances, of those
I can put a face to. With my eyes shut,
Squeezing the soft salts of their sweat, I see
Beyond my body, nerves, cells, brain, and leisure.
Blue coastal persons walk out of the haze.
They have outflown the wind, outswum the sea.
I think, and feel, and do, but do not know
All that I am, all that I have been, once,
Or what I could be could I think of it.
These blue pedestrians bruise the edge of me
To a benign remorse, with my lessons.
With my eyes shut, I walk through a wet maze
Following a thread of sounds – birdsong in
Several cadences, children, a dog-bark,
The traffic roaring against silence as
A struck match drowns it out, simple tunes of
An amateur pianist, a vulgar shout,
A bottle tapped against a thirsty glass,
The burst of its pouring, and the slip
When the chilled glass wets a wet lower lip.
I could not guess at what the pictures are
In the eyes of a friend turned round to watch
Shrub shadows dapple a few yards of lawn

As his smoke clings to his thoughtful posture.
Tonight, I shall look out at the dark trees,
Writing this in the muddle of lost tenses
At an o'clock of flowers turned colourless.
Then, as always, the soul plays over mind
With radiantly painful speculations.
I shall sieve through our twenty years, until
I almost reach the sob in the intellect,
The truth that waits for me with its loud grief,
Sensible, commonplace, beyond understanding.

A Summer Night

Dusk softens round the leaf and cools the West.
Rhythmical fragrances, wind, grass and leaves,
Fly in and out on scented cadences.
I go into the bedroom of the world,
Discovering the long night of my life.
This telephone is electronic lies,
Ringing with calls, with farewells of the dead
Paid for on credit. Nocturnal postmen ring
My doorbell; I refuse to let them in.
My birch trees have their own two lives to lead
Without our love, although we named them us.
They play inside the aromatic wind
That is their house for ever. Outside time,
On the sensation of a memory
I walk through the dark house, remembering.
I meet the seasons on the stairs, breathing
Their pulchritudes, their four degrees of heat,
Four shades of day, shade on shade, shade on shade.
I have gone through a year, in at one end,
Out at the same way in. Same every year,
But that year was different. I counted days
As Francis counted sparrows, being kind to them.
They were not kind to me. My floating life
Borrows its fortitude from a cool silence
Composed of green, from two trees, from the tingle
That was the touch of us against the world.
It left its lived heat everywhere we'd been,
A small white cry, one last wild, stubborn rose.

Listening

From the unoiled wheels of a bicycle
I heard a squeak become a human cry.
In those silent lamentations
When rose-petals fall, I heard
My sorrows murdered by aesthetics.
When laughter from a firelit barbecue
Travelled with woodsmoke across the gardens,
I saw an apple hold its skin against an apple –
Two blushing faces kissing in the dark.
In the orchard of listening fruit
Woodsmoke and voices crowded the foliage,
Rummaging for the sweet bite together.
I felt I almost heard the secrets of a tree –
The fruits falling, the birds fluttering,
The music danced to under coloured lights.

Reincarnations

The kitten that befriends me at its gate
Purrs, rubs against me, until I say goodbye,
Stroking its coat, and asking "Why? Why? Why?"
For now I know the shame of being late
Too late. She waits for me at home
Tonight, in the house-shadows. And I must mourn
Until Equator crawls to Capricorn
Or murder in the sun melts down
The Arctic and Antarctica. When bees collide
Against my study's windowpane, I let them in.
She nurtures dignity and pride;
She waters in my eye. She rustles in my study's palm;
She is the flower on the geranium.
Our little wooden train runs by itself
Along the windowsill, each puff-puff-puff
A breath of secret, sacred stuff.
I feel her goodness breathe, my Lady Christ.
Her treasured stories mourn her on their shelf,
In spirit-air, that watchful poltergeist.

Reading Pascal in the Lowlands

His aunt has gone astray in her concern
And the boy's mum leans across his wheelchair
To talk to him. She points to the river.
An aged angler and a boy they know
Cast lazily into the rippled sun.
They go there, into the dappled grass, shadows
Bickering and falling from the shaken leaves.

His father keeps apart from them, walking
On the beautiful grass that is bright green
In the sunlight of July at 7 p.m.
He sits on the bench beside me, saying
It is a lovely evening, and I rise
From my sorrows, agreeing with him.
His large hand picks tobacco from a tin;

His smile falls at my feet, on the baked earth
Shoes have shuffled over and ungrassed.
It is discourteous to ask about
Accidents, or of the sick, the unfortunate.
I do not need to, for he says "Leukaemia".
We look at the river, his son holding a rod,
The line going downstream in a cloud of flies.

I close my book, the *Pensées* of Pascal.
I am light with meditation, religiose
And mystic with a day of solitude.
I do not tell him of my own sorrows.
He is bored with misery and premonition.
He has seen the limits of time, asking "Why?"
Nature is silent on that question.

A swing squeaks in the distance. Runners jog
Round the perimeter. He is indiscreet.
His son is eight years old, with months to live.
His right hand trembles on his cigarette.
He sees my book, and then he looks at me,
Knowing me for a stranger. I have said
I am sorry. What more is there to say?

He is called over to the riverbank.
I go away, leaving the Park, walking through
The Golf Course, and then a wood, climbing,
And then bracken and gorse, sheep pasturage.
From a panoptic hill I look down on
A little town, its estuary, its bridge,
Its houses, churches, its undramatic streets.

Land Love

We stood here in the coupledom of us.
I showed her this – a pool with leaping trout,
Split-second saints drawn in a rippled nimbus.

We heard the night-boys in the fir trees shout.
Dusk was an insect-hovered dark water,
The calling of lost children, stars coming out.

With all the feelings of a widower
Who does not live there now, I dream my place.
I go by the soft paths, alone with her.

Dusk is a listening, a whispered grace
Voiced on a bank, a time that is all ears
For the snapped twig, the strange wind on your face.

She waits at the door of the hemisphere
In her harvest dress, in the remote
Local August that is everywhere and here.

What rustles in the leaves, if it is not
What I asked for, an opening of doors
To a half-heard religious anecdote?

Monogamous swans on the darkened mirrors
Picture the private grace of man and wife
In its white poise, its sleepy portraitures.

Night is its Dog Star, its eyelet of grief
A high, lit echo of the starry sheaves.
A puff of hedge-dust loosens in the leaves.
Such love that lingers on the fields of life!

Western Blue

The Navy groaned through its traditions.
Fats Domino sang "Blueberry Hill".
It came through a hatch from America.
The mothballed minesweepers pretended to be
A chorus line of the Western World,
Young ladies fallen into disrepute.

This dusk is that dusk, its perfect duplicate,
Down to the four swans, an evening mist
That turns the conifers to Western Blue.
They've closed the jetty down as "dangerous";
But I have nothing to lose, and I walk it,
An admiral of water, mist and dusk.

I waited on that hand of salty planks;
The air was the fingertips of loneliness.
A boy in the Valhalla of the age,
In an oily fo'c'sle, I listened to
Purred tedium in a Cold War anchorage.
My kit-bag was a pillar of salt with my name on it.

And I have turned to look back on a life
That has happened and died, most of it with mine.
Varicose barnacles have more grip than I have.
I take a salute of pine cones and lolly-sticks,
The flotillas of flotsam. Four swans depart
The way they did in 1957.

I hear the rhetoric of the depot ship,
Its propaganda filtered through
Its cups of radar, its mesh of aerials.
I shall transmit my elegies from here –
This station at the place called Western Blue –
A thousand messages beside the point.

Transblucency

A blue fog you can almost see through.
Duke Ellington

Transcending from the everyday
Routines of our mortality,
From blue to blue, and into deep
Sub-oceanic blue beyond the eye –
Diaphanous, soprano –
This sound portrays her life as one long rhyme.
Its nervous elegance
Calls with a woman's voice
In the key of serenity
That art is love, and beauty is
Our commonplace sublime.
Hear how it disregards injustice
For the intimate, for the lived,
For the pain of the species.
I play it again; I play it again.
Most nights I listen to aesthetic pain
Oozed through a black speaker,
Appropriate, uncanny, kind to me.
In autumn by the Tay when the geese are flying
I am a man remembering love
And the tune of her funeral.
The lights of Newport rinse in the tide,
Then one by one disperse, as life dissolves
Into the deity within ourselves.

A Rediscovery of Juvenilia

Dropped hairs spring as I turn the pages.
Old notebooks, old files,
A stationer's aroma . . .

A rusted paperclip has left its print,
Its mineral reflection,
On something I "sent out" twenty years ago.

They wave across my years, which are theirs also,
With their visible prayers
Returning down a paper echo.

Here is a poem in monosyllables.
Here is a meaningless adolescent rhapsody.
Here are the Olympic rings of a coffee mug.

This is an afternoon of perfumed panic.
A whiff of old jotters, and I'm a time-traveller!
Here, too, are pages of crossings-out.

Yesterday, a friend said to me in the street,
"Now that she's dead, what will you write?"
"Satires," I thought, "and long, inky romances."

Here, too, is a line, a lost one, that says,
"It is like listening to a rainbow . . ."
I'll close the book on it and start again.

Home Again

Autumnal aromatics, forgotten fruits
In the bowl of this late November night,
Chastise me as I put my suitcase down.
The bowl's crystal shines and feels like frost,
And these have been the worst days of its life.
Cadaver orchard, an orphanage of pips,
Four apples sink into a pulpy rust,
And *Eat me, eat me*, says a withered pear,
Pay for your negligence and disrespect.
A scent of Burgundy – a bunch of grapes
Drinking their mortuary juice, their wrinkled skins
Dwindled and elderly black emaciations.
My six weeks gone from home portray the days
On stopped clocks and a vegetable absence.
Throw out the green loaf and bacterial cheese,
Shrunk carrots and potatoes begging for earth.
It is very lonely on the green settee,
Under the lamp, with my breath visible.
The curtains dangle in a window-sway,
In window-cold. I touch their foliage,
Their textile, sympathetic park.
I have been there in dreams, walking among
Peach-groves, and dressed in raiment of the East
In vineyards overlaid with Martagon lilies,
Arabic gardens, the south of Summerland.
Warmth is beginning and the pipes shudder.
I taste my house. Each day of its hungry gnosis,
It led a life of its own, empty of me.
The moon's oasis, the moon sipped the fruit
And the dust settled and thickened, the cold
Entered books and furniture, china and cushions.
My open suitcase mocks me from the floor.

The room is an aghast mouth. Its kiss is cold.
I think of a piano with its lid locked
And a carved, ivory silence in it.
I look at a vase. It is too much to bear,
For it speaks of a deranged expiry,
An accusation of browned leafage.
I see the falling off of its petals
In a flashback of flowers, the white zig-zags,
A snowfall of botanic ecstasy.
A spirit shivers in the appled air,
And I know whose it is. A floral light
Bleaches my eye with angelophanous
Secrets. They are more than remembering,
Larger than sentiment. I call her name,
And it is very strange and wonderful.

December

"No, don't stop writing your grievous poetry.
It will do you good, this work of your grief.
Keep writing until there is nothing left.
It will take time, and the years will go by."
Ours was a gentle generation, pacific,
In love with music, art and restaurants,
And he with she, strolling among the canvases,
And she with him, at concerts, coats on their laps.
Almost all of us were shy when we were young.
No friend of ours had ever been to war.
So many telephone numbers, remembered addresses;
So many things to remember.
The red sun hangs in a black tree, a moist
Exploded zero, bleeding into the trees
Praying from the earth upward, a psalm
In wood and light, in sky, earth and water.
These bars of birdsong come from another world;
They ring in the air like little doorbells.
They go by quickly, our best florescent selves
As good as summer and in love with being.
Reality, I remember you as her soft kiss
At morning. You were her presence beside me.
The red sun drips its molten dusk. Wet fires
Embrace the barren orchards, these gardens in
A city of cold slumbers. I am trapped in it.
It is December. The town is part of my mourning
And I, too, am part of whatever it grieves for.
Whose tears are these, pooled on this cellophane?

Snow Days

I

Professionals have all gone home –
No need for medicine or law,
No need for numerals or rhetoric.

A white sabbath of the mid-week.
Each grey window has its person.
The trees are wintry, Netherlandish brushwork.

I can feel history close
Its bedroom door. It reads,
Then switches the lamp off.

II

Our mouths dream of each other, all lips.
The lanterns ahead of us are all at sea –
Green, blue, red and yellow, the lamps of Avalon,
The fictions of a life that is to come.
Snow melts on the waters of *insula sacra*
And lit peaks look like a stone regatta
In the fantasy of distance, in Yondertown.
Plash of oars, the warmth of love-furs,
And apples in the terraced orchards are
Already drawing juice from the wet wood,
All summer's sugars in the frozen ground.

III

The minstrelsy of oak
In a thawing grove. I turn my cloak.
White, legendary white
In a birkenshaw,
Moonlight and silver birch
And the song of a snow-bunting
Says that the time is here
When wolf, bear and the big cats
Shake their extinctions loose
In the dripping forests.

IV

Snow is its own country, and it beckons
With its white finger crooked, and is calling
From the hush of its chilled bulk, its tons
And territories, its white ground falling.

White penitential gardens of snow
Are where I meet you at a chosen spot
Somewhere on the ice-miles. I do not know:
Is this our story or its counterplot,

Here on the nothing? Androphonos, '
O Aphrodite Scotia, the white rain
Squanders its wet on us, and we shall cross
Seas of upholstered ice and not complain.

The Stories

No longer are there far-flung outposts of Empire
   Where a heartsore widower could command a wall
Against the hairy raiders ignorant of commerce.
   Too much morality has interposed
Its wishy-washy journalism and hope. Who am I
   To weep for Salvador or Kampuchea
When I am made the acolyte of my own shadow?
   Grief has its own romance, its comedy,
Its preposterous and selfish gestures. Men and women,
   Who, one day, will feel as I do now, I
Empty my heart, my head, dreaming again of days
   Gone by in another life. I could sail North
To Spitzbergen, to the iced-over mountainous islands
   Outlined on charts of the glacial deltas,
Or south to the rainforests, or to the blank of sands
   Drifting like the heartlessness of time.
Where is the frontier I could serve with a paid sword
   Dutiful to an imperial ass who lavishes
His days on orthodox, abstruse theology
   And his exchequer on a paradise
To please the gluttony of his heretical consort?
   At my age, I could die splendidly on
A staircase, unarmed, banished, but soldierly, before
   The spears and sabres of the wicked host
That trumped my preparations and stole the city
   In the name of their Prophet. I could have died
On the trails of exploration, under the sun or the arrows.
   And what religion is left now, to serve
With local Caledonian sainthood, stern, but kind,
   Baptizing the baby Africans, and plodding
To a discovery of God and waterfalls?

Nor are there any longer those unvisited isles
Where a beachcomber might scrounge a boozy salvation.
  To meditate in a tropical hovel –
Palm leaves, creeper, coconut shells, jettisoned
                                  containers –
  On wheretofores, buts, ifs and perhapses,
Over that anguished prose of what we think we deserve,
  Or don't deserve, but live with, either way,
Would be a perfect if anti-social philosophizing,
  Doubtless illogical, or arrogant,
Or windily puffed-up to heights of self-deception.
  Interior ethics, like oncogenic catastrophes,
Happen anywhere, the melanomas of the sun
  Or the occult surprises of contemplation.
Why grieve like this? I loathe my bitter, scorning wit,
  This raffish sorrow artificed by stories.
I can see myself in a jungle-drunk's smeared linen suit
  Under the fan in a lost trading post,
Most Maugham-ish in my matutinal repartee
  At my breakfast of mango and whisky
As the steamer arrives, delicate with white nuns
  And crates of Haig and quinine, the new clerk
Already mothered on the rack of a malarial fever.
  There are a thousand plots in the narrative
In which grief is the hero. In these frequent stories
  There is always somewhere to go to, outbacks,
Exiles, White Men's Graves where piratical gun-runners
  Mix with evangelists, where wilderness
Brings out the worst of men as well as charity,
  Where sacrifice embroiders every tale
And the devoted nun weeps in the shot-up pagoda
  As a Chicagoan's lung-blood soaks her arms.
Breast-plated with Gustavus Adolphus and Dalgetty,
  I could have lost myself in Baltic syntax.
Foot-slogging the Sahara with kepi, pack and gun,

I could have made the beautiful gesture,
The joke of spitting in Death's broad, fictitious grin.
  It is no longer the world of the stories.
Opportunities for a ludicrous public service,
  For the lunacy of last-ditch duty
To Monarch, regiment or John Company,
  Are stoic options stored in Yesterday.
Why be discreet? A broken heart is what I have –
  A pin to burst the bubble of shy poetry,
Mnemosyne revealed as what, in life, she stands for.
  I shall observe the moods of the great sky,
The flight of herons, the coming into leaf of birches
  And the religious glow on ancient waves
Breaking against *Candida casa* of the cliffs.
  If you should see me, or one of my kind,
Looking out to the far ocean from a lonely headland,
  Or walking by the hedgerows, then turn away.
Walk on by, and leave us there to remember and dream
  Our speculative visions of the past
Narrated through the legendary, retrospective fictions,
  Tales of anachronism. Such days they were!
Not even that sweet light garnishing Sisyphean innocence
  Redeems me, dedicated to the one
Pure elegy, looking as if I like the way I am.
  I do not; for I would rather that I could die
In the act of giving, and prove the truth of us
  Particular, eternal, by doing so
Be moral at the moment of the good death, showing
  An intimate salvation beyond the wish
Merely to die, but to be, for once, commendable.

Anniversaries

Day by nomadic day
Our anniversaries go by,
Dates anchored in an inner sky,
To utmost ground, interior clay.
   It was September blue
When I walked with you first, my love,
In Roukenglen and Kelvingrove,
Inchinnan's beech-wood avenue.
   That day will still exist
Long after I have joined you where
Rings radiate the dusty air
And bangles bind each powdered wrist.
   Here comes that day again.
What shall I do? Instruct me, dear,
Longanimous encourager,
Sweet Soul in the athletic rain
   And wife now to the weather.

Glaswegian starlings fly
In their black cape, a fluttered noise,
Ornithological hurrahs
From spires in the November sky.
  The Candleriggs is husks
And cabbage leaves, a citric scent,
A vegetable sentiment,
Closed apple-depots in the dusk's
  Indigenous metaphor –
Arcadian orchards of the lost
On this Bohemian sea-coast
And exits, pursued by a bear.
  I passed our wedding day
Drunk on the salad street, a null
White-out of loss and alcohol;
Your ring, our anniversary,
  And starlings in my soul.

A liquid light sips dew
From how it is as blossoms foam
With May's arboreal aplomb
Against a reminiscent blue.
    Day, number, memory,
Kissed hours when day's door hangs ajar
And light crawls on the calendar,
Each routine anniversary
    At night, and noon, and dawn,
Are times I meet you, when souls rinse
Together in their moist reunions.
Iambic, feathery Anon
    Opens anthologies,
Born and reborn, as days go by
In anniversaries of sky
When oceans cradle little seas
    That water in the eye.

My diaries are days,
Flesh days and real. The calendar
Recurs to tell us who we are,
Or were, to praise or to dispraise.
   Here is a day come round
Again. This window's a wet stone
I can't see through. Daylight and sun,
Reflectionless, a glassy ground,
   It slides on vitreous space.
I shiver in the memory
And sculpt my foolish poetry
From thwarted life and snapped increase.
   Cancer's no metaphor.
Bright rain-glass on the window's birch
This supernatural day of March,
Dwindled, come dusk, to one bright star,
   Cold and compassionate.

Hush

Shh. Sizzle of days, weeks, months, years . . .
How much of us has gone, rising and crying.
My skin seeps its pond of dew.

Air sips and licks as I walk out today
In the transparent jaw of the weather
When the first leaves are greening.

Behind me I can hear
A click of fantasy heels,
But there is no one there.

She is with me, as I call to see
A sick friend whose skin is drying
On the bones of her spirit.

I stand on the sad threshold with my flowers.
How old this is, and how the heart beats faster
As I wait at the bell like a mourning wooer,

As the dog barks, as I give my flowers
And a secret wind blows in from eternal woods,
As my flowers sigh, asking for water.

Leaving Dundee

A small blue window opens in the sky
As thunder rumbles somewhere over Fife.
Eight months of up-and-down – goodbye, goodbye –
Since I sat listening to the wild geese cry
Fanatic flightpaths up autumnal Tay,
Instinctive, mad for home – make way! make way!
Communal feathered scissors, cutting through
The grievous artifice that was my life,
I was alert again, and listening to
That wavering, invisible V-dart
Between two bridges. Now, in a moistened puff,
Flags hang on the château-stacked gables of
A 1980s expense account hotel,
A lost French fantasy, baronial.
From here, through trees, its Frenchness hurts my heart.
It slips into a library of times.
Like an eye on a watch, it looks at me.
And I am going home on Saturday
To my house, to sit at my desk of rhymes
Among familiar things of love, that love me.
Down there, over the green and the railway yards,
Across the broad, rain-misted, subtle Tay,
The road home trickles to a house, a door.
She spoke of what I might do "afterwards".
"Go, somewhere else." I went north to Dundee.
Tomorrow I won't live here any more,
Nor leave alone. *My love, say you'll come with me*.